Luxuries of Grace

Tom Radzienda

Luxuries of Grace

This book is a *Sovereign Word* Publication

ISBN 978-616-305-851-5

CIP 55-23166

Preface

When writing poetry, I'm searching for wisdom within myself and in our world. I seek the primordial source of truth, penetrating to the roots of existence. This search has taken me all over Asia, Africa, Europe and the Americas, as well as into the quarry of my own being. The search involves *Vipassana* meditation, fasting and spiritual healing. I write feverishly until I discover the answers for which I yearn.

Poetry comprises a lifetime of self-discovery. Once written, I recognize my personal vision and beyond; I tune in to universal awareness by abandoning a personal perspective and merging into a sense of infinity. I hope my poetry serves others seeking to discover themselves in extraordinary ways.

Luxuries of Grace portrays those phenomenal moments when we are completely present and mindful, absorbed and harmonized with nature as it eternally spreads before us, pure and essential in our true Sovereignty.

These Luxuries remain virtually ineffable even after writing hundreds of poems and explaining the concept to as many friends. This mirrors the essence of *Taoism*: the *Tao* transcends all explanation. This irony typifies the paradoxical nature of this compilation; its only possible language is poetry.

This collection presents a daring balance between transcendent Luxury and Grace juxtaposed against poems that vacillate between violence and lyricism. I seek to preserve a profound sense of equanimity as I explore the rich dimensions of existence.

As you're reading, you may be arrested. That is, you may question the Grace of poems such as *Music by which to Destroy the World* or the anarchistic *Bicycle Tour*. These poems may not sound 'Luxurious' or 'Graceful' to your ears, but they represent genuine exploration through the labyrinth of becoming. This poetry emphasizes authenticity, whether that implies droplets of morning dew or drops of psychological blood.

My personal path for the last decade has involved discovering where poetry meets healing as represented by poems such as *Healers and Madmen* and *The Healing of Poetry*. I've been writing poetry for more than thirty years. I increasingly recognize that the intuition, images and symbols in poetry parallel the work that I perform with *Reiki*. In both pursuits, I am seeking wisdom and wholeness. In poetry, this involves insight and epiphany. In *Reiki*, it's referred to as attunement and healing. On this topic, my book *Personal Transformation through Reiki* shares numerous perceptions and healing experiences.

Poetry, like *Reiki*, began for me as a very personal quest and has expanded into a global community service. Writing and sharing this work has been a tremendous healing for me – therapeutic in every dimension. I hope you will be inspired by this experience as it nurtures your insight into Luxury and appreciation of Grace.

Many thanks to all my family and friends who have supported me in the preparation of this collection and helped me comprehend the diverse experiences that the poetry entails.

Tom Radzienda
Thailand

The Armless Weaver's Transcendent Loom

The homeless poet wanders across the universe
In search of the signatures of every friend
That has ever joined the regal parade

He witnesses the birth and flowering of time,
Its dispersal, its infinity,
Its inheritance of illusion.

The secrets of the jungle are woven from the absence of time
Into the intimate tapestry where eternal history
Expresses its deepest wishes

In the ebb and flow of the armless weaver's transcendent loom
Colours are cast and patterns drawn.
All who approach discover their image

Exquisitely reflected in the endless cloth:
A mirror, each to each,
Draws homeless poets ever closer

To inspect the intricate details,
The destiny and dust,
Of every thread entrusted to the loom

Its great waterwheel spinning in perpetual motion
On God's chosen river

Luxuries of Grace

Luxuries of Grace reveal
The elegant hand of love that transcends reason
Bringing the universe to the very edge
Of time where now we compose
Presenting the world in all its glory
Breathing life through the trembling leaves of a whisper tree

Enigmatic shadows fall across the dale
Beneath the colonial bridge
Invisible songs of autumn singing from upper limbs
Cold rippling waters drumming the humble stones
That shape the river bed
Great gifts beyond what we deserve
Beyond measure

This warmth where the sun falls
Breaths of crystal air
Colossal trees looming over their shadows
Minuscule hummingbirds on the cusp of nectar's tongue
        Dogs at play with hints of creation
                Berries, friendship, a kite's own wind
                        And the very sound of your name

                        – All – magic – all – Luxuries – all blessed

Gracias.

The Soul of Music

Music, her soul revealed in the wind
Bathes naked in the elegant morning breeze
Tempted by the warmth of a promising cup
Of coffee and the rising sun
To emblazon the spirit of the universe with *crescendo*

She pours fragrant water over the nape of her neck
To exorcise the demons of misbegotten melody
The baptismal acid splashes on the barren earth
Nourishing an original species
To blossom into esoteric song

Men and women labour at brass and strings
Trying frantically to comprehend her prodigious compositions
For the wind is privy to the inner mechanics of music's soul
Just as the sun is intimate
With the sensuous body of every chord

She tickles pianists through the epochs to match her wit
They perform tantalizing leaps through gymnastic innovation
Catapulting across keyboards,
Jumping generations with chaotic faith
Towards where the future has yet to be emboldened

They place their Grace notes
Between her majesty's breaths
As she winsomely sighs with admiration
That a planet might dedicate itself so intensely
To the supremacy of her soul

The Loneliness of Truth

When the voice compels me to my humble knees
No alternative exists to all encompassing silence
Just before a lonely bolt of lightening strikes me
Deepest where I am weakest
The truth tests my mettle

Could modern life
Be meaningless diversion?
       So much construction of egos and fortresses,
       Bank accounts and publications,
       Names, addresses and bulwark memories
       To extinguish the inferno of loneliness that burns within

What, then, if all we've ever accomplished in this life
Is nothing more than concrete and insulation
To barricade ourselves from cold, winter dreams
That endure long solo nights
Lonely stars singing wistful songs
To the only ear in the universe able to bear
The unequivocal, nocturnal, frigid truth:

That lonesomeness is the only sure state of existence
Dependent neither on the will of another
Nor the wisp of any wind

Sovereign Word

What remains of our divine right to be?

What happened to our ability to perceive
Beyond the shadows cast
By stately illusions?

Unfettered by titles and degrees
Unencumbered by papers
And documented trails

We
Are
Sovereign

Streetscape, La Paz

Daughter with mango spread across her hands and cheeks
Son, freshly plucked daisies in either hand, pink and white
Girls after school sprawl across the brass inscriptions
Of the roundabout
A man without fingers, without hands,
Holds between his forearms
A plastic flute, determined to survive

Searching for peace in every street vendor of pineapple,
Humintas tamales, whipped cream,
Mellow biscuits, car horns,
Vivid green vests of security
Boys, some deviant, some not yet
The sun elapsing behind the Bolivian Andes, *La Paz*
Los frios, the cold, imminent night
Hawkers, hot, sexy cinnamon, *api morado*, if we can find
The woman in the shawl on the hill;
Humanity before and after dark

Saw a blind man on the corner
Thank God for my vision,
For my hands and fingers and the musical gift that flows,
For lovers strolling down cobblestone lanes
Children chasing pigeons, thank you for the gift of flight,
Gift of youth, the pony tails of daughters nimbly woven
By the maternal fingers of elegance, gifted by the universe

Here on earth, I weave my existence
Across a gaggle of continents
Abide by the culture, language and law of each

Bless this diversity, this training for the epic journey
Through the infinite universe
I shimmy my earth-worn soul seeking
The present world in my arms
Its embrace as of my love
Discussed in the circle of dreams,
The ice cream and flower market,
Coca leaves,
All performing their celestial moves on the streets of *La Paz*

Every touch is evidence of the glory beyond the human edifice
The seer pierces the ambiance like the bull horn
Of an urgent bus approaching humanity at fire speed
Foretelling the light that aims to bless
Providing vision and wisdom when we penetrate
The veil that cloaks us all like the Incan shawl
On the erstwhile shoulders of the *Quechuan* woman
Captured in the urban lock

The breezes in which we believe
The force of gravity, speed of light
Black holes, light years and Big Bangs
Quantum physics and nuclear spaghetti, believe
We are made to believe;

Release,
And ask beyond these frontiers what is behind it all,
Beyond the primeval call to duty?

Enter the deepest cell of your being in noble, honest silence
Be present with the source as it surrounds you
In any earthly manifestation you perceive
Impregnated in the core of every whisper
This is only the beginning, the trial run
Before the universal marathon en route to *The Peace*
Beyond the reach of our leprosy ridden city

Connect the words on the page like stars in the sky
Create a cosmic vision more replete
Than any cinematic gander at the truth
Reach and connect to the grandeur with all the fortitude
Of our eminently gentle souls
So painfully buried beneath our social grit.

The drunken man shits his drawers, but remains kind.
I cannot explain.

      If you have sufficient words to describe
      How much I love this passion play
      I will kiss your hand,
      Let you this pen,
      And beg your explanation

Alien Rhythms

An irresistibly irreverent rhythm
Weaves its way through this soul
Unencumbered by the weights of the city
And the dams of the river
Leaping free from the gravity of the urban drum
Seeking its own measure and peace
Its own evolutionary definition

Piercing deeply the inner universe
Pulsing pumping pulsing piercing pushing pulsing
Beyond barriers into the unknown river
Weaving waxing waning
Warping into the ether
The here and now
Luxury of Grace
Of the planet's soul

The Dust of Violins

Time for silence
The lull between notes
The pause
Between
The movements of the symphony
When the audience coughs
And wayward curls
Are neatly tucked
Behind ears;
Tangible anticipation
Of the fiery passage
On which the violins
Will soon embark

Sit on the edge of the strings,
Knowing that we, too
Will be sawed to pieces,
The dust of violins, floating
Gently and rhythmically
To the pit of the orchestra

To reflect on what we are:
The Silence

And the noise:
That we are not.

The Inverse-Square Law of Gravity

Loneliness is the power to deny gravity
Pulling you down, first to your knees
Then flat to face your centripetal pain
Sweeping the squalid floor where the roof has always cried

When gravity begins to fatigue in defiance of Newton's laws
Dragging you down becomes an exhaustive chore
Gravitational leaks seep first at the public edge
Until full blown scars burst at your hidden seams

Then gravity scatters randomly, hopelessly
No longer abiding by universal laws
But wiggling and shimmying
Like an abandoned child in a darkened universal hall

The dominant forces of the universe are content to play
Electromagnetic and nuclear forces cease to obey
Gravity in its vacuous state seems unqualified
To bring the planets back together again, as it once

May have been on a peaceful Sunday afternoon
Before fear drove you to Europe in search of anti-gravity
While denial opted for Asia in hopes of inner sanity
Tearing gravity between indecisive poles

Could Newton lay down his once proud gravitational claim
To be constant throughout the universe
To admit, finally, that perfect constants are a neurotic trap
Whose doors are only now beginning to unbolt

Revealing the grave
State we are in

The Current of Knowing

This man long lost on waters dark; choppy
Distracted by promise of emerald islands
Deceived by the devil's smile

What words could a poem express to heal the craft?
To explore and repair the scars of its wounds
After so many years of piracy?

Golden yacht hijacked;
Sabotaging the essential course
The captain too hungry and blind to nuance the subtle change

He sails towards the sun; 1° of error in the arc of his course
Multiplied by the sum of his years of diversion
Leads him to a desert where words neither fathom nor float

Where waves neither rock nor roll and why?
For which desert befits a boat with sails
When water is not in its nature?

In the absence of words,
Which waves might weave existence
Into the current of knowing?

Healers and Madmen

Healers and madmen wander these crumbling streets
Haunting the *chocolataire* with half a dozen dogs in tow
Smiling and whispering as they climb
To the temple above the village
Astutely aware of the freshly minted breeze
That feeds every living soul minute by minute
They speak with more colours than those marketed on earth
Whisper melodies beyond the range of human ears
From dimensions beyond the human eye

Madmen and healers laugh and are laughed about
They exemplify the glory of paradox
Their every sentence begins and ends with a smile
Madmen heal the planet with such gentle steps
That shadows shudder with unfathomable envy
Healers trace surreal lifescapes on the earth
Escaping from fingers pointing towards madness
Begging reason for patience
To understand the world beyond our ken

Healers and madmen wear extra jackets
To surmount extraterrestrial cold truth
They wear long hair and grungy beards
To weather the blizzards steeping their souls
Laden with experience
Their wisdom is not synonymous
With social convention or empirical proof.

When you press the horizon; it bends to fulfil your wishes
Touch the heart; it heals madness of its own accord

The magic of things that we have yet to comprehend
Need not be hastily denied

Vision is Poetry

It is to share, that we seek friends
To see, that we stand tall despite the danger
To love, we risk the pain that our camouflage
Will be revealed, and in the darkness of the truth
Buried, we breathe our heraldic vision

On the plains, step up my friend
Gather the jungle and savannah among your memories
Breathe as the eagle, brave in its dreams
Fierce in its search for fulfilment
Yet lacking anger even as it devours its prey

Your vision is poetry that seeks through darkness
Revelling in the finest truth that has sifted
Through desert storms harassing your eyes
But your mind is a transparent gem
Where the dream of evolution reaches its crest

While love whispers its poetic song

    A gazelle pauses in mid-air

    A giraffe nibbles on the silent melody

    This continent is blessed with our love
    Perceived through painful tears across the sea

The Apple of the Story

Each endowment is presented on a silver platter
For you to accept into your life
As within the core of the Apple
Resides the source of fruitful truth
Once she arrives within your bouquet
She opens and blossoms

Her wisdom penetrates every corpuscle and vein
Until you absorb her cosmic vision
Gathered over the millennia of orchards
Bequeathed from seed to fruit to soil to seed
And finally to bleed
Within your arteries to nourish your roots

Luxuries manifests in your life
Many more than accountants can fathom
The gift of the walk, the sharing, the talk,
Our daring, our time, our caring, our rhyme
Through which the Apple of the story
Releases its butterflies like messengers to the earth

To remind you; here is your souvenir:

> Regale in every breath, every smile, every kiss,
> Every falling leaf, every mile, every death
> That you be invited once again
> To the nucleus of the universe
> As it manifests in your divine heart
> And permeates your being

Luxury has fulfilled its passionate duty
To enlighten you:

> The butterfly performs her sacred dance

This Morning's Cup of Tea

Every drop of water
Flowing through the Sacred Valley that nourishes my home
Is a Luxury; for what essence of her faith
Have I ever truly earned?

A sip from the glacial spring
Inspires fluid consciousness
Cherished not today during our reign of industrial grit
But appreciated in the lull between the construction of dams
And the toxification of cancerous streams

Hiking through the eastern valley above *Urubamba*
I'm surrounded by a parade of children
Who bless me with their greetings
We mingle at such a pace, set by four-year-old Maria
Taking fractional steps towards her family home
Her entire hand gripping my index finger

We stop myriad times along the dusty trail
To know all the neighbours who live
In the basin of *Chicon* glacier, that I,
Consecrated by children's mountain innocence,
Completely forget that I set out this morning
To discover the source,

> The frozen chunk of truth slowly melting
> Its oldest, innermost secrets
>
> Into this morning's cup of tea

Quantum Search

The mind
In search of truth
Seeks, questions and queries

Does mind recognize that awareness
Is the universe –
In search of itself?

Painter on the Esplanade

The painter
She
Sits on the Esplanade every night at 6
Colouring the sky with remnants of blue - sky - sea - grey
Indulging in the vast orange array

She
Paints for hours the details of seconds, painting
Passing, fading, feigning new light as she transforms old
Sunshine elapsed since she spread the canvas
Wider than Borneo, steeper than sky across the universe

Always a fire in her heart, the vigour of her flames
At this hour, in the corner of the page
She
Defines time through her capricious brush, with love
Like a comb through her evening hair

Tenderly as only a woman - only a painter - she
Ascribes an atmosphere, each nuance
A tropical smile or aging shades of wine - she
Portrays each twilight's cinematic breath

Words transform into sunrays and clouds - or ripples
On the ancient South China Sea, stirring
The paint in her bucket,
Eddies at her feet

Painter on the Esplanade (continued)

Power bursts forth as her beauty
Stampedes across the sky
Riding
Transparent
A stallion
Galloping
With banners as time races by

White clouds enamelled like porcelain dolls
Swirling like a child's innocent top into oblivion
Between the blue spaces of yesterday and tomorrow;

She knows. She paints. She describes for the world
The purpose of her vision, to behold, no -

To partake - in *maghrib*
The evening prayers of a descending sun
Elsewhere on the rise – she paints

She loves.

Listening to the River

Listening to the river and reading
Between the splashes and the stream
What the paternal hand has offered us,
In flowing disguise; the secret of existence

Reading the sun's final request as it approaches the horizon,
Exhausted, it would seem, to these chilly stones, outstretched
Shadows, these fallen leaves; but the glitter on the river is ever as
Golden as the locks of the angel whose fire assures our destiny.

Is it some secret esoteric language
That so few understand the sanctity of water
Unable to appreciate sacred space
Wide enough to spread our souls across the lawn
Without being trampled by industry

A yellow-breasted warbler takes flight

Memory Wavers high in the Andean Breeze

Tall reeds of ancient straw
Sung golden by the God of the sun
Whispered pale by winsome night

Each, a memory, terraced with granite
Blessing the carnal, snaking *Urubamba*
River, flowing secretly, silently, below

Through the Sacred Valley at *Pisaq*
Whisper the unknown grains, in peace;
Listen to moss and lichens painted with Grace;

A civilization stretches for centuries
Beyond these colours
Whose sky remains anonymous

Bicycle Tour

กรุงเทพมหานคร

I may have been born a sleeping, half-dead dog lying in the gutter of *Ratchada* Road, my eyes bloody, half-cocked towards death, towards you, or

Fate may have suggested that I be a speed bump on a perilous road, where it would be I that slowed down the cars to save the lives of the children.

Had destiny rudely played her cards, I could have been born a political fart in Chomsky's linguistic underwear, lingering long enough to speak more truth and intelligence than your daily dose of CNN

If chance had determined a different path, I may have been the dusty red cap on a toothless old man, smiling as he pedalled his garbage cart up the down side of his own mirage, at odds, somehow, with the over-sized lorry ready to cement his remains

Had luck been differently rolled, I would have been born as tobacco in a government cigarette, taxed to their liking as you smoke, and I, a tender toxic puff, would secretly lodge myself somewhere deep in your windpipe and manifest myself decades later, first as a nuisance cough, then as full-blown cancer, and when your relatives gathered at your gagging, choking deathbed, I would be reborn in their tears

In a springier variation, I might have entered existence as a bungy chord, strapped around the automotive paraphernalia in the boot of your car and on one road-side night while repairing a flat, you would reach for the jack and I would seize the opportunity to release years of tension in a single, swift left hook, gouging you in the eye and leaving you to bleed, bright lights racing by as red tears fell

Bicycle Tour (continued)

I may have been bred, had the tables thus been set, the dull knife of a butcher with too much zeal as he carved the life out of a pig for the convenience and delicacy of your next bowl of noodles as you slurp them into your mouth

I may have been appointed a bright life as a safety cone, on the honour role, neon orange in my proud grin as I bravely warned of danger to come, until some drunken fool ran me over, flat, and burst my egotistic spine

In a thematic variation, I could have incarnated as a bald tyre stuffed obese with concrete until I was heavy enough to support a weather torn umbrella in the poverty torn slum of *Huay Khwang*, keeping the sun off the shoulders of a plump little woman selling the bloody carcasses of slaughtered chickens

Many are the variations among random probability; were I born a silver bullet sitting alone in the chambers of a *Smith and Wesson*, rouletting my way through life in poignant anticipation of entering the left temple of a stubborn skull

As genetics was to have it, I was born and raised the personal bicycle of an anarchist, cycling the unnamed lanes and dirty canals of a primitively modern city, searching for what?

Answers to questions of existence and fortitude, tyre pressure and traffic lights, lost rainbows, sudden storms, typographical errors and sore butts.

White Rose of Friendship

Call her the white rose of friendship
But she is better known as eternity
Nowhere else but on this thorny branch
Could such a gentle scent linger so close to the edge of fear
As the universe unfolds
Following its own transcendent logic

She mirrors every earthbound dream, petal for petal
Reminiscent of intimate friends
Grown, wed and enthralled by all the portals
Through which she intends to pass
On her matrimonial journey
With the son of the celestial gardener

She is surrounded by flowers in a rural bouquet
Collected just as another rain prepares for its hour of duty
Her colours are defined in the trade as yellow, pink and white
Yet each is a separate galaxy
Putting forth its hard earned hue
With honour, compassion and finesse

The ears of the roses wiggle
Like a hundred loony puppies at the promise of a smile
Wild petals whose landlord is too often forgotten
Liberate their joy beneath the provincial sun
As friends gather to spread the nutritious endowment of love
Across the gardens of earth

The Signature of my Soul is a Poem

The soul be such
    Essence

Of delicate invisible fruit
That to paste a label
Or hang a name
On its lapels
Would violate
Its eternal elegance and Grace

Hard to explain
In a world where names
Are chiselled into buildings
Hung on trees
Collared on the necks of dogs
Barbed with fences across continental plains
To foster the perpetual illusion
That we understand
    By knowing the name

When Flight Chose Birds to Grace the Skies

When flight chose birds to Grace the skies
And represent Her Majesty in ambient view
The clouds and mountains conspired
That eagles and doves would never succeed

Until mountains peaked through the misty wind
To perceive the wisdom of flight proven true
On the first wings Gracing currents across the valley
Where effortless charm tilts its wings with a grin

The lush green velvet hills of *Coroico*
Assemble on the edge of the Amazon
Admiring her Excellency's gospel truth of flight
Each bird a tribute to the divine light

Lifting wings higher than human vision
The elegance bestowed on the planet transcends capital truth
To Earth, I ask forgiveness for my trespass
To Skies, I kneel in eternal, suspended awe

I trust I tread gently on this soil

Wildflower

The wildflower seeks most
To remain unnamed

Music for Flamingos

Listen to this song; once you touch its melody
You will never smile again
Until you hold your breath
And whisper the tears
That have long anchored your soul

Then the melody, like a Serengeti flock
Of flamingos, begins to flap her pinkened wings
Waiting for gravity to release
Its almighty grip on her bones
As she elevates, in defiance of the influence of earth

Measure by measure, she sings
While your own soul is scaling G, A, B, C#, D
Your very own musical signature emerges;
However you spell your tune,
She removes the grief

The notes, in alphabetic orgasm, surge
Into the air, wings beating frenetically
Pain, exhausted, lifts beyond the pall of silence,
Into Beethovian tomes where symphony
Raises the pressure of your blood

Music for Flamingos (continued)

You will never cry again;
Neither to douse the flames of earthen hell
Nor lube the gears of God's great shredding machine
Where all songs, after singing, crying and completion
Are shredded into razor sharp scraps a hundred miles long

As she paints morning sky over Tanzania
Your heart is dipped, brushed,
Splashed and dried of every colour
Until African dawn is thoroughly
Painted across the equatorial sky

Raise the Ancient Rainbows

This is why you were dragged here
From the comfort of your university laurels
To a remote mountain in sacred Perú:

      To awaken the ancient rainbows
      That long ago faded into oblivion
      Through colonial neglect.
      It is your task to restore the colourful banners of light
      Long darkened in mentally polluted caves
      Hidden beneath scattered ruins of the Inka moon

      Shine your sword and dispel the myths
      That modern humanity
      Has broadcast over its mind
      Respect each ribbon of the prism
      Celebrate the myriad hues
      That emanate from the caverns of Andean temples
      Pouring sacred wisdom into Amazonian springs
      To nurture the people of the plains

      Raise the ancient rainbows!

Whispers from the Inkwell

What metaphysical breeze
Embodies the elegance
To bless poets and artists
To splash quintessence
Between questions?

Who speaks the breathless voice to the inner ear?
Who's tickling the keyboard of consciousness?
How do we divine intelligence that guides us?

Who opens all the windows of our hearts
That transcendent wisdom speaks to us
Even after our futility and war
Our depressions and poverties
Our hungers and disgrace?

Still the voice bestows higher gifts
And goals for the fallen race
Music always dreams of a saviour

Craftsmen and saints assemble novel visions
The breeze whispers through the brushes
And inkwells of human artisans
Trying desperately to interpret the fabric
Of the celestial dream through their subtle touch

    And remain sane enough to portray
    The colours for the masses
    As we slave for subsistence

Where Born the Wind Was

Where born the wind was
    Patagonia
        I don't remember
            I can't forget
                Where born I was
                    Or home was how was

Nation's language
    Beyond religions
        Where born my soul was
            Patagonia
                I don't remember
                    I can't forget

Drifting mountains
    Where born my soul was
        Floating islands
            Pink flamingos
                Where soul my birth was
                    Not knowing nation

Not breathing culture
    Or singing freedom
        Just silent watching
            Where born the wind was
                Poplars swaying
                    Patagonia

Dance I the grasses
    Wild flowers
        Turquoise waters
            Argentina
                Sweeps born the wind waves
                    Grass dance the song lives

Just wind the grass does
    Birds ducks and geese are
        Rippling waters
            Mountain bluescapes
                Sweeps of daisies
                    Floral dreamscapes

Aqua savannah
    Hover seagulls
        Where soul my born was
            Blue springs from mountains
                Where born my voice was
                    Singing questions

Am I he who?
    Where born the wind was
        Patagonia
            Southern temple
                Dream the hawks of
                    Amber bushes

Strolling friendship
    Rounds of hardship
        Where goes the wind does
            Kaleidoscopic
                Soul of the mystic
                    Patagonia

The Hardest Stone
Ollantaytambo, Perú

Exploring monuments of history
Inspecting footprints of opinions
Solid granite is carved
Into obstinate stones
With carbide chisels, claws and rasps
For all to bear witness

But what stone is supple enough
To change its notion of tigers or lilies
When the season changes?

Opinions are a fortress
To protect the vulnerable soul.

Who might safely approach me with courage to speak
Lest the guards of my dungeon come out at arms?

Better saunter away from the prison
And wander the countryside between towns
Cross raging rivers on loopy swinging bridges
Clamber up hills of cacti, mines of salt and ancient wonders
Than sit enthroned
By the menagerie of beliefs
I defend with adamance

As the sun weakens its hold on my stumbling corpse
I fall full weight on the native cactus

      I can only smile,
      Laugh, and count my wounds

Sustainable Breath

The Buddhist cat crawls into my lap
And rests her head on my wrist
She scratches her white furry cheek on the nib of my pen
Encouraging me to not be industrious,
Not merely how to avoid multi-tasking,
But how to discard the entire cult of productivity

"Sit here," she teaches, "take a soothing breath like me
Twitch your nose and attend keenly to your senses
Don't be bothered with barking dogs and unwashed linen"

"Purr," she says; the feline *Om*

This Luxury of stepping beyond time
To open the windows of the world
To the radiance of mountain morning

Letting the dust of night settle where it may
Marvelling at each breath as it lifts my belly

Each breath,
In tacit recognition of the laws of impermanence
Settles into a silent lull at the root of my being

Fire on the Edge of the World

To love the sky, and blue, and sharp blades of summer grass giving, beneath my feet, lupines of sacred violet, Antarctic breeze, replete, and you

Love the sun, its birds and geese, monarchs and serfs, rabbits and hawks, mirroring lakes, barking dogs;

Me, sliding down a muddy slope the day the snow betrays the summer sun in my arms, complete, and you

Mushroom from the rotting log, pine from the corner of the garden, timbre our hearts, sever our hemispheres.

The *yin and yang* of seasons, reasons, hearts, clouds, skies, mountains and seas on the sacred *mesa*, herself, divine child of the forest, balancing the eagle's wings across the spectrum of our full being, in love,

Blossoming, like no other star, stable like no other mountain, spring forth her dazzling bright cold *bleu* winds of time upon our fate, cold *azul* glaciers embrace our feet, our eyes transfixed on her southern pole on which she spins all of humanity, all these species, these dandelions and gems, these Graceful acts of creation on her index finger, spinning

Life, like no other love, blossoming ever within the heart, the eye of the southern daisy through the endless parade of our consciousness, we, barefoot,

Grace *tierra del fuego*, fire on the edge of the earth.

Om-niscience of Green

The song of green and a bamboo flute
An ancient twist tree embracing itself
In time, whose children are birds on the wing
Whistling songs the colours of the Rainbow Mountains
In accord with the Argentine sun

Waning into a winter whose flavours are dreamt by ice creams
While parakeets and arrow birds interweave their melodies

Seashell chimes percuss in the *Pumamarcan* breeze
Waiting, within the wisdom of *Om*

With the coming breath emerges
Om-niscience of the green

The *yogi* in the sun takes flight in dreams

A yellow balloon bounces its brief existence
Down the chalky orange cobblestone

Wiry poplars shade the voices of vendors
Whose shawls dance every ribbon of the rainbow
The tapestry whose every sound is a blessing

Music by which to Destroy the World

I compose a fiery ballet where dancers
Kick in the teeth of the audience
Who take it in turn to homicide

Their blood is printed on musical staffs
Tainted by anger and angst; in which key
Is it suitable to compose such a melody?

By wit's end, the orchestra will have bowed
Itself into a spasmodic, climactic heart attack
Resounding with fire through the neurotic piccolo

The world, in which we have been scored,
Our lonely little lines of courage, lost in a barrage
Of basses and tubas far larger than our heaviest burdens

March, to death, this world which has strung
Me along as I search for a rhythmic pace
To release me from the conductor's gaol

Into which I have walled myself
Through petty paranoia and
Stampeding insecurity: The strings assail

Music by which to Destroy the World (continued)

My heart; the conductor's baton is sharpened
To orchestrate my eviction; no solo
Tonight, the poet has been erased

From her own composition. The sounds of emptiness
A wooden hall, centuries olde,
Curtains taught like kettle drums, dust

And despair sprinkled into every timbre
Insufficient breath for the winds to bleat
Or the pianist to beat any more sense into the

Tune. She will soon go deaf.
The plaintive cries of the final violin
Will perplex only the sparrows too blind to seek

A warmer home. She will not forgive.
She will not love. The score must decry.
An unfinished symphony in honour of my demise.

The Poetry Season

In cold weather of heroic despair, I beckon you
To read the poems our friends have often shared
And warm your hearts with gentle thoughts of us
As we stand by your side to keep you strong

In hot seasons of elegant joy, I summon you
To write a poem to share with all these friends
Who stand by you on slippery paths
Cheering as you strive towards your goals

In times of loss, the stones of the river are not ashamed
To lay bare beneath relentless rays of sun
For their strength is in their bond to each other
Shaping the destiny of the river

The rainy season shares its soul to fulfil the river
Our memories flow through the river as it transforms
Times we have struggled to touch our spirits
To be students of the poetry season

The waterfall knows it must leap but for a moment
Then, considers itself a river or a stream
Until it spreads across a barren field
Waiting for first flowers to bloom

Faithful Silence

To hear the eternal song of the universe
Requires infinite silence of the mind

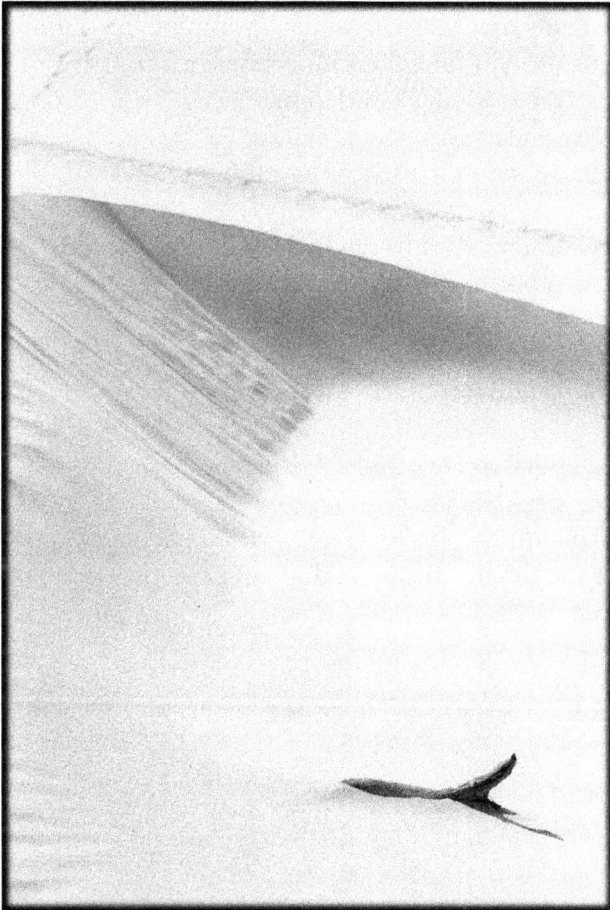

Song of the Andes

The song of the Andes grips the village
Marching and swaying
Whistling and drumming
Its traditional path from foothills to the plaza
Down market road through the soul of the *pueblo*

She commands me with a hammer drumming the seminal beat
She charms me whistling through echoes of bamboo
Invoking music from ancient depths,
Present here and now,
The song never written, the music without end

The procession winds through frigid mountain streets
Every twisting body craves to be vacant
As music commands the limbs
Leading each dancing drumming human vessel dream
Through the eternal rounds of the sacred song

As it unravels its mystery through repetition
Shrill reeds from the jungle
Kissed by the human breeze
Empower mountains to rise in glory, in tune
Leaving our spirits in suspended awe

The Poetry Market

Poetry abounds from drawers and shelves
Unfiled, spewing forth wisdom and misery
Destined for a market that defies my ontology

Crawling from the wreckage of a thousand broken odes
The grey-stubbled man treads gently on piles of rubble
So meticulously destroyed during the revolution

Creating a new spirit within the confines
Of a gradually aging corporeal stance
He stands taller now in every stanza

Glancing across fields long left fallow
During the searching and destroying of years
Now so fertile, willing to yield whichever fruits are sown

The seeds take root, sentence by sentence
Each heart aligns itself with a fresh universe
From which to perceive the evolution

Of thought that has come thus far, proceeding
To lead us gently by the warmth of his hand
Pursing the vision that shines within

Within the Empanadas

In the ecclesiastical shadows of *Sancto Francisco*
On the corner of *Córdoba y Caseros*
Sitting in a cheesy *café* at the sticky table
In the corner near the window
Making *grandioso* decisions concerning *café y empanadas*
My feet hotter than the streets
From the duration of an aimless stroll
To places witnessed, forgotten and lost
Like afternoons sorting a menagerie of thoughts
Over the drama that life pretends is purpose
And what hearts silently describe as desire
The *café* is rich, frothy and hotter than ancient shoes
Leaving only the *empanadas* to be served

On this first afternoon sitting Graciously still
Beneath northern Argentinean skies
Bluer than the pride of their national flag
Clouded white not by any doubts
But by the offspring of Andean rains
Abandoned here at a thousand metres
Hovering between Atlantic and Pacific waves, loved equally well
As they shape themselves into corporeal dreams,
Floating with a Colombian sense of flavour
Speaking for themselves with rain when opportune
Publishing puddles and urban streams
Of consciousness when the mood occurs

Within the Empanadas (continued)

This might be the sort of *café* where Jesus and his disciples
Would congregate before a sermon
Of love and neighbourly demeanour
Or where they might stroll for a snack after a searing sermon
That uncompromisingly penetrated worshippers' souls
Who for their part learned to smile in response to any pain
Knowing always the crystal anchor of truth
Within ravenous waves of existence

My part, in the corner, off stage,
Is the assembly and disassembly
Of the paradoxes that enlighten me
Which I savour as I tune to the visceral chords
Of my own chaotic love

Murder Variations

Murder was just another variation on the art of suicide
Painted on another man's face in response to the mirror's pain
We revved our engines and sharpened our knives
In the race towards perfect execution; at ease

With death more familiar than honest pain
Hidden at the bottom of the blackest barrel of paint
Unstirred, unscraped, left to harden the arteries of emotion
Denied long before this body was ever conceived

The blood predicted to flow should suffice
To buffer the tears we never figured to produce
So the salty blood shall nourish another generation
Conceived in honour of the family illusion

Why must we wait in line for the axe to fall
On our stubborn greying heads
When bullets are cheaper by the dozen
Even if I require just one

To Nurture the Children of the Sun

Fire sweeps across the hemisphere
Blessing mango and orange with vivid joy
Night crawls from beneath the secrets of dusk
Blanketing the sky with deeper mysteries
Displayed in the enigmatic stars
Whispering their astral hopes to the universe

Silence, but for crickets and echoes
Of human feet on cobblestones of darkness,
Resembles the whisper of searching hearts
Stepping quietly from thought to thought
Guided by the light of finely woven breaths
Lighting the path one step at a time just as eternity presents itself

Follow the reciprocal silence between heaven and heart
Inhale the evening ellipse of time and space
Exhale silent tranquillity simmering in the lungs
Sustaining the human body for another prescient interval

    The dance of now between the universe and I
    Meeting where silence is our most precious melody

Return of the Unshaven Poet

Is this any way to return?
>Words marching through the rusty pen
>Like songs through a musical cadaver

Abracadabra: Smile, a word becomes a phrase
>Gentle rhythm simulates an evening rain
>The poem searches for a razor

To shave off the dust of un-groomed years
>A vest to complete the literary wardrobe
>Where will it find shoes in style?

This new-found fever for poetic flavour
>Follows a thousand-day linguistic fast
>Where no words were allowed to flourish

Emerging from beneath the poverty of ink
>Greyer, yet more agile
>To what melody will it sing?

A Little Death for Everyone

Soon
I too will stagger out in the midnight
Of an unfinished moon,
Naked as any dog barking at his unseen fate
At a velocity faster than anyone comprehends
I too will lay in a little pool of blood and pile of threads
That once held me together

I too will whimper and moan
Bite you or anyone who comes close enough
To perceive the truth of my bones,
The sacred tears of my blood
The river of sadness that pours forth
On the dusty country trail
Unpaved but for unrepentant futility

Then I, in my flopping throes,
Shaking off tears of death
Like the fettered bug struggling to be free
From the bondage of the spider's web
Each caught in the drama of their race,

I, painfully and oddly mis-tongued
Misfit to any nation or race
Caught in this body's spider web of desire
A human cadaver in a world so inhumane
Upside down and bloody
There; the knife that carves my seizured heart
Wrestling with anacondic tendons of existence
To be free of the thoughts that surround me
And the emotions that embalm me

In the Heart of Silence

A gallery of perplexing emotions here in the heart
Where thickets of bamboo grow so tight
Weaving impermeable filters to test
The mettle of the sun, here

In the heart where ancient timber lies at the cusp of memory
Unwilling to fade, unable to stand
Solely waiting for the untempered passage of arboreal time
To wither away the bark and bones
And soften through a million leaves
The screams of agony echoing the hysteria
Of lovers many midnights after the fall

A grove of cinnamon trees sprouts in the continental heart
Gnarled with sinister crannies that veil the ephemeral scent
Attracting bounty hunters for centuries
Tramping through restless, uncaged jungle
Where tears rinse away footprints
Wile away scars

Cinnamon truth never tampers with time
Keeping ever to herself
Regenerating the dust of fallen leaves into the soil of birth
Where shadows are masters of deception, yet never tell lies

What is the Essence of the Universe?

Awareness of itself

To Shine, to Be

Silence all these hidden years
While the pen waited in a broken hand
Biting my proverbial tongue
For fear of disturbing the silent truth
Before whispering the inaugural word

Rejoicing, this voice begs
Permission to share, to colour your dreams
With insights of mountain jungle desert stream
Into your heart I request admittance
To shine, to be

The Confidence of Summer

Visit each perception
      Witness every green leaf
      So confident in its summer hue

Believing the breeze
      To be an eternal lover
      That will never fade

Allow each thought to fall
      Like the autumn leaf
      That will not survive tomorrow

Moments of Balance

During exceptional moments of balance
Between sanity and rhythm, standing
In a crowded underground train, swaying
From *Rama 9* to the *Cultural Centre*
Rocking back and forth between love and friends
We persevere, only to be judged by uncertainty
Between good and evil, and the impossibility
Of a terminus station; forever
Abandoned between destinations
That never actually exist but in name

These moments are transcribed into our steps
Escalating at once into written similes
Evolved from freshly surfaced smiles
As we emerge from the underbelly of the streets
Never yielding to setting suns, hurried critics
Or the ethereal elegance of roads polluted by terror
We awaken from our subterranean progress
To ponder the indecipherable patterns of urban transit
Subversive in its crawl through cities
We never intended to make home

The Nudge

May we nudge the universe
Asking for inspiration –

    A little thunder and lightning
    A chaotic spelling bee
    A lunar mooning
    A deep black well of boiling ink

To describe our little haves
And chagrin our little have nots

Or must we beg from the sidelines
For a pad of paper and a few drops of psychological blood
To scribe the events of the day
And note the calibre of hearts

As they pump their primordial jazz
All across the horizon

The Genetic Piñata
Part One: The Laughter

Thank you for the rope
It's truly one of a kind
And certainly suited to the purpose

Let's hang this infant boy, trembling with petrifying frustration
In his wrinkled, cotton Chinese 'jammies,
From the rafters of the living room

Then beat him with laughter and jokes
You've been collecting since you were abused
Amused now as you finally ratify the legacy

Beat him like a multi-coloured *piñata* that swings
Helplessly and erratically from a string
Beneath the clubbings of eager rivals

Until he finally goes up in smoke
Releasing decades of unrequited anger
Bursting shrapnel on those of you

Unfortunate enough to have not yet died or moved away
And sufficiently close to face the fatal detonation
Of toxic venom, where candy might have been stayed

Let aunts and uncles crowd around in their '60 'dos
Laughing and jeering in neurotic anticipation
Of their '70s suicidal dues, to release

The cancer that is caned on his sagging cadaver;
Deride the boy until he hurdles across the ocean
Running eternal marathons until he slumps, exhausted,

Unidentified in *Lumphini Park*
      beneath setting sun and banyan tree
Unable to stand, let alone piss into a cup
To measure the concentration of insanity in his urine

Bleeding childish babble from his maligned nose
To release his cerebral haemorrhage
Long held at bay by liquor and dope

Waiting for just the moment to explode:
You should have beaten me with sticks, at least
To impair me with permanent bruises

That I might verify the veracity
Of the ancestral pain
That resides within my battered soul.

The Genetic Piñata
Part Two: The Legacy

While each of you stayed the white-haired course
You planted the genetic *piñata* in each of your kids
That their future children might also join the charade

Who, when they least suspect, on the cusp of middle age
Step on the land mines of our lineage
And the venomous curse of a century of generations

Bursting into the faces of the crowd
Like poisonous candy at a terrorist parade
Killing the ones they love, or killing the ones they're with

Harp of Autumn

Autumn opens its heart to reveal
      The bounty of colour held within its awe

We are lured into the silence of crystal blue skies
      Whose breast embraces the depth of our souls

Water of the sacred mountain trickles divine
      Tickling forth sounds incumbent in every stone

Music streams through the fingers of the fall
      Its rocky rhythm beating in accord with our hearts

What hand have I in this glory,
      In this Luxury of creation?

What mind have I in this music,
      In this festive Grace?

What song sing I in natural magic,
      In humble silence?

Whose words are strung on the gently falling leaves
      Of the autumnal harp?

Flowers and Stones Weave Colours for All

Flowers and stones take sides
Concerning the impermanence of fortitude and Grace
Each island daisy grows with equal patience
Beneath the primordial sun
Surrounded by the cosmic lake of the Inkas
Higher than the masses of civilization
That labour below in their industry

The sun powers the aged wrinkles of sacrosanct waters
Nourishing flowers, eroding stones
Extinguishing illusions painted
Since beauty and Grace were first memorialized

These stones, avid chroniclers of geologic time
Gather the sun to bake evening dreams
While flowers, bashful by fate
Lace solar colours into their petals
To impress the night
And assure the wind continues to recite their names

Flowers and stones among all the lovers
Have come to the *Island of the Sun*
To touch the soil and prod the balance of tastes
Weaving colours for all
Existing but once
In a lifetime of infinite lessons
Each a wrinkle on the face of the western slope
Waiting for a simple summer
Glimpse of a robin's winsome song
Before the wind whispers it all away

Fire Burns, not Knowing

Fire burns not knowing the destiny of its flames
Knowing only the hot apparitions of arboreal souls
Whisked from the corners of history

Fire dreams of Jazz, *Ellington* and *Davis*,
Coltrane and *Fitzgerald*,
Each on the frontiers of ethereal genius
Bowing only to the sun in the magnitude of their fire
Dreaming they are the inferno
Burning, without hearing the destiny of their songs
Only the presence of a cryptic melody
Embroidered into the lace of their souls
Gracefully selected from the urban noise and evolved

Exhaled through brass and nuanced from strings
Echoing through the woods and winds of the present moment
Never knowing whose ears will tune in
Whose will go deaf
Whose will be indifferent to the inner fire
The vital force of the forest
The primordial gold in the heart of the quarry
Of the universal mind
Just out of range of the saxophone's enigmatic dreams
Into vast channels yet to be plucked
Not yet tuned by delicate fingers
Dreaming of the sun
The original fire
The song
The fire
The sun
The poem

Silence is Wiser than Thought

Silence of the stream
        Is the wisdom of a vision
        But the stream never whispers
            Her secrets always deeper

        Than the bubbles of her laughter
            When tickled beneath the ripples
            Of the gravity
                That carries her along

Silence but the stream
        Does not write any sermons
        As she casually delivers
            From her mother to her child

        All the silence of her words
            Beyond the capture of a pen
            Steeped in noisy obsession
                Narrating the silence of her game.

Silence is wiser than thought;
        Carry me to the river
        Where the children of the stream
            Are quieter than the whisper of the leaves

        Teach me - silently - to be the stream

The Healing of Poetry

Grace arrived at the shaky wooden table
Overlooking the ancient cosmos of *Cusco*
Thoughts flooded my skull as wily as Noah
Writing a snappy ark of observations
To commend the mountains on their linguistic verve
The tablets of prose arrived more quickly
Than Moses could calculate
Spilling from stones into the dusty soil

Healing arrived
In a transcendent voice that sought to soothe
An exhausted empty page:
The curative voice of the primordial mountain king
Painting, healing or singing
In accordance with the skills of the transcriber

A painter divines via the language of colour and shape
A healer is guided by probing silent intuition
While a singer takes note of melody and chord
Each in their way transcribing mountain wisdom
Into their respective uncanny crafts

To heal, sincerely surrender illness
Just as to experience visceral feeling
Truly forgo obsessive rationale
Leaping, in both cases, into the essence
Where all is balanced and in tune, where
Poetry and healing become synonymous

As we reverberate in the chambers of the healing poem
Energies from quantum to celestial
Are silently organized by the *maestro* of the orchestra
Tuning and timing our beings
In relation to our mission

Poetic senses, unleashed from the protocol of rigid reason
Respond to the symbols of the highest peaks
Comprehend the thunder of river and sky

In healing as it is in poetry
Open from root to heart to crown
To receive with confidence and joy
Inspiring wisdom of mountains
Literate long before the glaciers and the floods
So we in our dusty chilly corners might abide
By the *Apu*, mountain intelligence
Whose wings are of the condor
Whose roar is of the puma
Whose infinity represents the coiled serpent

Unifying the universe within the stanzas of the poem

Secrets of the Acorn

What are the secrets of the begging child
Sleeping among rats of decay?
Have you seen the boy with remnants
Of some long forlorn scabby meal
Shovelled without tutelage into his hungry face?
What does he speak of the human soul
Long since fallen, like the oak
For which his barren village was named?
These vessels of life, each in their kind
Contain the wisdom and folly of every preceding generation

What are the secrets of the acorn
Sleeping among the tattered relics of fallen trees?
Agony and pride of eternal memory
Of all that once stood elegant in this denuded village

Have we fenced ourselves behind barbed oaken fences
And the steel gates of bugless, dirtless communities?
Where no poor child would ever tamper
Let alone claim any civil rights
Not to dine or bathe in Luxury
But simply to perceive the beauty that blossoms
Beyond the forbidding gates
Or simpler yet, to stand, to simply be
A dirty faced boy with one open hand
Eternally asking for the debris of privilege
To sustain his round of alms
His trivial stature inherently speaks
Of another world, itself gigantic
He but the tiniest flotsam floating
Asking to reveal that Grace and disgrace
Be perceived in their knotted elegance

Secrets of the Acorn (continued)

The acorn, I invite tonight to rest on my *Patchakuti* altar
Bringing its vision to my candle-lit chambers
Guidance along my dusty trail of destiny
Beyond any name, she, acorn, loves, trusts me
To guard and replicate her deepest hope
That humanity not fall into ruin for lack of Grace

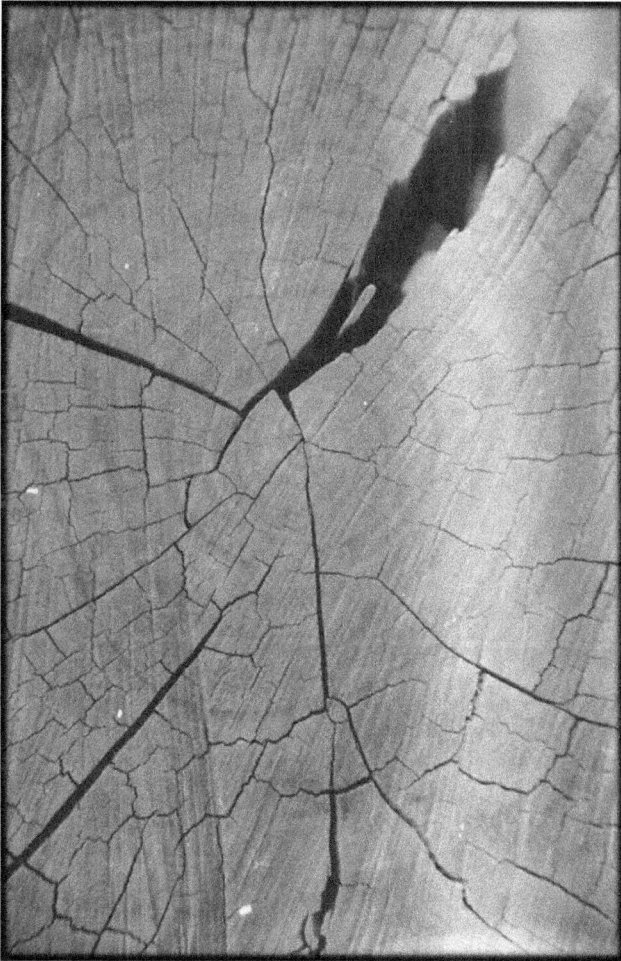

Tears of the Sun

The stream where sunlight engages a million bubbles
Deeming each one home
For a moment, until each one sings
Its infinitesimally brief elegy
Before bursting into a tear,
Flowing, its evolution complete,
Into the southern arms of autumn
In the sierras
Of consciousness

The bed of stones bathing naked in the stream
At the afternoon's foreclosure
Rinsing free from a day of colours ever on the wing
Beneath three bridges promising the mountain chapel
Where Grace is evidence of a fallen tree bursting with green
Despite its roots upended by the wear and tear
Of seasons on the soil
On the shores
Of consciousness

Where golden leaves express their final opinion
Of the grazing sun

Patching the Roof

I remain diligently attached to the swinging
Rope as I approach the ceiling with a bucket
Of pitch to patch the holes worn right through
The tarpaper roof, crucified
By a previous generation with 16-penny nails
Hammered deep; the very weight of existence and time
Has sheared the shingles from the original facade

Bloody drops of satanic rain permeate the beams
Seeping through an attic of cast-off family luggage, dripping
Into every fibre of this dying living room
Where we collect our puddles
Father left through the front door, to die,
Leaving the roof so patchy
Mother ran out the back door, to hide, leaving the rafters bare
I, slung like an orphan from the caboose of a runaway train
Embrace the rope of my adolescent chores
Frantically patching the ceiling's despair

I paint my predicament on your patient ear
Tar dripping, hot and caustic into my face and hair
Sealing in forbidden tears to restrain the intruding rain

Come with your roller skates when it's all over and we'll
Roll off the roof like precocious brats
Leaping corporeally into the wired teenage thorns
Of a childhood we were condemned to miss
Landing in the barbs where flowers absorb our blood
While the sky douses rain on abandoned dreams

Divine Song of Morning Birds

When birds sing to the silent morning
Transcribing archaic melodies of dawn
Granted by the Grace of Andean breeze
Across these deeply breathing mountain ranges
My private ears gather intricate secrets

I ask myself, my friends, all of you
Have we, in our most silent noble minds
Ever truly heard the morning song
As it whistles and entices its way
Through the prison walls of heavily guarded consciousness?

These birds, free without declaration
Weave delicate wisdoms across the morning sky
Denouncing the arrogant drones of those
Who wield their cunning saws in the felling of trees
Denying the universe its precious songs

The last surviving timeless heart
Revels in the ancient melody of rainbows
Before colours were bound by names
Sing, morning bird
Dream your ancient heart

The Lexicon of Innovation

Poetry is the creation of a world
Uttering ineffable words with enchanting tones
Employing innovative lexicon while handcuffed
Inventing backwards and forwards on a tightrope

Strings of thought on which to hang our hats and hearts
Engineering petals that metamorphosize
Folding themselves into everything they were ever denied:
      Undefined, unrefined and tempted...

Challenging the scriptures of dictionary –
That prison for definition
That nastily twists barbed wire
Around the artistic curves of our cerebellums

The poem, exasperated by convention
Leaps from the page and persuades
Truth from the writer to elicit
A humbly chaotic response worthy of blood

Then, each nominated thing that sheds
Will discard its name:
      Robins and willows, whispers and dreams
      Tigers and waltzes, peaches and cream

Each in their turn blossoming
From the pilot light in their eyes
To attain mystical stature:
      Namelessness that honours no bounds

Unleashing an orgasmic breath of life
A river of light into dark craniums of fear
Condemning empiricists' favourite antiquities:
      Definition, categorization and quantification

Death Wish of a Stillborn Soul

What is beauty?
The question plagues and haunts
Those who ask themselves,
In the silent stillness of being.
While the same question
To those who have never asked
Is the death wish of a stillborn soul.

Inherent in the asking resides the dream
The Luxury of evolution
The query is perpetually posed
Earning a confidential response
And then it wiggles free
Like a minnow from a rusty hook
Refusing to play his life as bait

Ask again a soldier
Struggling free from a fatal bayonet
Whose wound spills not just beauty
But bleeds the splendour of truth incarnate
For coming generations to ponder and gaze
With instinct in their blinded eyes
And bruises on their souls

Grizzly in the Closet

For those of you with cats, dogs and parakeets in the home
A grizzly in the closet
Might seem a bearable inconvenience
But you have never witnessed the havoc a grizzly wreaks
On the soul where he seeks asylum

Do you know the grizzly propensity to wrestle the night
In your sleep, leaving you exhausted at dawn?
Grizzly lapses back into hibernational comfort
While you struggle between yawns
To convince the rest of the world of your sanity

Grizzly provides warmth on winter nights, but at what price?
He arrives in the dead of sleep to snore heavily in your dreams
Shaking you awake to play his ursine games
He seeks comfort through nocturnal hugs
Suppressing any hope for deep breaths and supplementary sighs

Should you hypnotize him into mercy or force him outside
To starve him of his own narrow diet:
    A man's lonely secrets and twisted fears
    Baseball cards, comic books and yellowed newspapers
    Knotted up, bundled and stored in the closet of brooms

The bear could easily roam the vast enclaves of cold memory
But he prefers staying close to the hearth
With the solitary love that tames him
Embrace him; he is your warmth, your love, your pride
He is you; and all your life bestows

Peacocks within Stone

Find a place in the hills above the *pueblo*
Seek a shady little alcove beneath a tree
Lean comfortably on a massive rock where you can
Neatly weave the strands of distress that entangle your heart
Into a mat of silence where days can be sat unencumbered

Be the bounty of life that flourishes within your reach:
A sturdy old whisper tree that keeps his opinions to himself
A gnarly, penitent shrub
The slender grasses of nature's prom
Plaiting their own carpet of repose

Beware of the Bushes whose burrs like leaches attach
To every cell of your existence
Allow the breeze to empower the gist of your thoughts
Be wary of clouds that push their own agendas
And resist their persuasion

A bird is hidden somewhere within this maze
A peacock in every stone

Memories of the Sun

In the gardens below the chapel
Flowers advance towards wisdom
Visions reach forth

With the autumnal rise
Of an increasingly reluctant sun,
Pour the poignant rays of life
To which every creature
Wills its dance;
      First and last;
            And every song in between.

This long song of a season's magical touch,
Composing infinite colours
From the chatter of parakeets
And rustling gold underfoot

Proposing Grace for the feet and wings
Of all who respect this minuet.

Even for stones that rest inert
These songs are duly treasured
Basking in the memory of the sun

Where the sun falls
A man sits beside the river
A shadow of sophisticated wisdom
A silhouette of consciousness

Knowing that nothing
Can truly be measured;
Only experienced.

Thorns of Scrubby Existence

Patagonia scampers every hour to the ocean
To sooth her scorching feet
She sits on the shore for millennia
Soaking her blisters to remove
The thorns of a lonely, scrubby existence

Gazing across the sunlit Atlantic mirror
Observing her gritty reflection
Pondering her rocky gulches
Endless stretches of abandonment
Human encroachments into her oily heart

The infinity of sun that she has hosted
The frigid winter nights that she has harboured
Half a continent to herself
Yet not one sibling in whom to confide
Confessing only the scratches and tracks of her inhabitants
Etched eternally on her grizzled skin

She listens patiently to oceanic shrewdness
She reveres the texture of geology
Tampering with her Grace

History admires her intimate relations to the blue
The shadows that always probe, but never pierce, her serenity
All her noble enchantment;
Her mystic knowledge of distant stars;

She eludes human imagination

A Fresh, Bloody Shave

As if a fresh shave could remove
Years of deception
With a steaming hot bath and brutally sharp blade
I could trim to a sheen
The age of forbidden devotion

As if beneath the grey and white portrayal of age
Lay innocent the smooth vegetarian skin
Of an honest, humble young man
Bent more towards fidelity and truth
Than bloody lies dripping from his chin

Posing under the weight of tolling chimes
Renamed and retuned to prevent the tarnish
That otherwise collects on the brass of war
Conducted in hearts behind the melody's face
Masquerading behind whispers, whiskers and tears

By what account could Grace leave the face unscarred
By razor marks jugularly close to the breath
Long accustomed to swerving around the truth
Leaving tell-tale hairs at random angles
More familiar with denial than regret

Love is welcomed back to its original roots
While smiles rage vibrantly
Blood stains the crevices
Drying in un-ironed wrinkles
Where only sweat could revive the stubble

Waves of Silence on the Island of the Sun

Silence. Silence.

The chaotic mind can never discern
Subtle clues of existence that ripple with gentle persuasion
To conceive beyond the dimensions
Of a busy city mind enthralled with entrapments
Of money, time, cars and a menagerie of distractions

Busy busy busy noisy noisy noisy
Silence silence silence the mind
Master it with mute observation
Sample the sweet blue waters of the wisest
Freshest lake embraced by the Bolivian Andes
Cold, rippling sounds of perpetual depth
Echoing its own aquatic history

Each ripple is a life observed
Released like an immature trout
Unleashed; the hook aims to ensnare
While the silent monk of the infinite pyramid
Beneath the sacred glacial water sits, one breath,
So calm, serene, persisting for millennia
Eternally breathing in, breathing out

Silence brother silence mister silence *señorita*
Silence my friend silence.

Waves of silence are too delicate
For the measure of urban mind
The inner spirit must awaken to detect the primeval Buddha
Respiring deep beneath fathoms of history
Beyond rigid knowledge of human intellect
Into the serene
Ancient nautical gem
Parent of all colours and wisdoms
Sibling to silence
On the shores of the *Island of the Sun*

Uncanny Mutations of Comprehension

Dimensions; the pyramid multiplied by itself
Presenting the seminal cell of being
Hexagons/circles, facets/feelings
Thoughts parallel/oblique penetrate the body
While soul unknown/unnamed/denied wonders

"In what dimension might I be measured?"

The corpse breathes, shaping/persuading/cajoling molecules
Into clusters of belief, solidifying into organs/concepts
By which to brainwash; cross-lateral journeys forbidden
Cage this beast; this uncanny geometric/psychotropic mutation
The poem materializes in the end; the end.

Silence between the Leaves

The Latin morning sun
Finally arrives
To salute my hibernation cove;
       His heart long since acknowledged
       But his smile long over due

Shadows that inspired morning meditation
On the silence between the leaves
Lift their cloaks in eastern retreat
Leaving me overly sweatered under solar auspice
Now fully in plough across the *azure* Andean sky

This is the sacred labour of intuition
Ever present
Ever open
Always on the prowl for mysteries of Grace
As they manifest in earthly scenes

       A stream roars with laughter,
       A willow touches her toes,
       A dozen ears flicker on half a dozen dogs,
       Wind chimes covet attention
       So much song to sing

The sentient soul
Absorbing the quintessence of morning Perú

Geology's Infamous Gaze

Where travel vagabonds west to California each night
Through the arid Mojave desert
Just their skins and bones
Crumbling stones beneath their age

Sleep vagabonds in dusty, faded gulches
Dry with the wrath of millennia
Nameless souls tucked into caverns and caves
More fitting rattlers than men

A wanderer so scorched fits in well
Where death sleeps beneath the sun's steely raze
Where vagabonds write self-scribed epitaphs
Hoping to come to terms with destiny

Vagabonds only know the path as it's revealed;
They come to rest, sure as stars
Beneath piles of rocks wildly tossed
By geology's infamous gaze

Weathering

Wandering are the springtime children
Youth's very own vision
Grown tall and searching heaven's meadows
Lost in the maze of lies weathered on their souls

Gone are elders but for photos
Uncles and fathers have taken leave
Early departures for unknown heavens
With friends, victims of the casual erosion of time

Elapsed like summer
Into the yellowing foliage of its own family tree
Chopped for tonight's last hope fire
Warmth before the cold bite of autumn devours its final meal

Faded are the magical colours and whispers of hair,
Hardened muscles and swiftness of feet.
The aches and pains of winter stumble forward
Dusting their dismal flavours on the feathers of wings

Our effervescence flattened by neglect
Along with dissolution of national integrity
Dissolved in the urine of its own infected bladder
Spilled caustically on the parchment of an unexamined cult

Its last few words
Drip on the tiles of a sordid toilet floor

First Quote of the Future

The comeback after years of drought
Doubt having sucked the legs right off the words
Castrated the tentacles that used to know
And now, but for silence, return

Resuming not in political heat or economic diatribes
But guided through language on wings of silence
Not the quietude of despair or the angst of expectations
But the invisible whisper of a season, changing heart

Words release the tension of contradictions
Indifferent to direction or drive
Neither callisthenic nor Olympian aims
Just a murmur noble enough to rise above the threshold

Scribing to discover, not to prove

Barren Soil

Loneliness is that human condition
That has covertly justified
Every endeavour of our species

Bent, ever more like a gardener's hoe,
Towards self-destruction
Tilling barren soil, seeking

A solution to the desolate soul

When to the River

Can I walk unfettered through the autumn leaves?
Breathing the chilly mountain breeze and
Be, just - simply walking being -
Not on a path or crusade
Not coveting insight, simply -

Walking be, unattached to the illusions of my own grandeur
Unsure of the boundary and depth of my being
Never certain whether I am on the path or the incarnate path
Being peace as silently as dusk
With neither reasons nor goals, purely -

Smiling be, not materializing the mystical realm
Just accepting, being here
Neither proving nor denying
Decreeing nor decrying
Righting nor wronging, merely -

Gentle be, in silence - knowing by smiling
Teaching by listening, learning by sharing
Equilibrium without measure
Every sense firmly contoured within and around me
In the absence of self, solely -

When to the River (continued)

Silent be, the autumn breeze whispering
Secrets of death to morning flowers
Caressing golden leaves still on the branch
Fluffing the thinning hairs still on my head
Lifting birds too feeble to seek a warmer sun, wisely -

Honey bee, eternally in the now of life
Where no compass could point to the truth.
Only rivers know the secrets of the mountains;
When to the river, autumn leaves
And every lane is painted like a walk-in Renoir

Ineffable Grace

Poetry, in its primordial quintessence
Is unconcerned with beauty, love or rhyme

In its seminal impetus to exist
Poetry wrestles an irresistible urge
To hover

With ineffable Grace

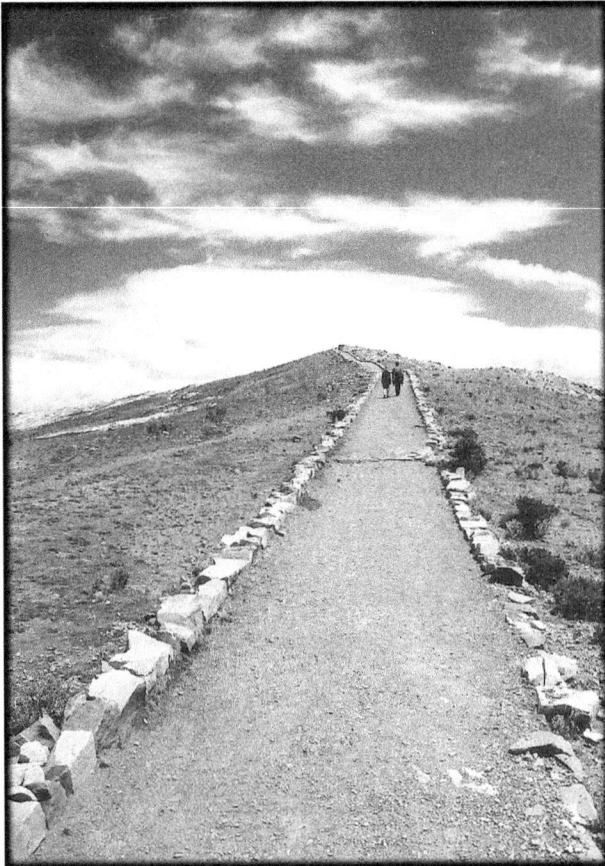

Being the Poem

Rendered lame by science and facts
Handicapped by history and thought

How might I prevail over the prisons
So my soul may once again rise?

To dream the fire of the butterfly
Sing the chorus woven by cicadas

Dance the jungle's rhythm
Hear the ocean's enigmatic charm

Reaching the full potential of union
Oneness with the world, with the word

Being the poem

Violent and Lyrical Embrace

Only the emptiness interests me at all
The empty pages waiting for the blood
The vacant room patiently waiting sombre tears
From vacuous eyes lacking focus, steering
Into the unmapped days of our absence

Hugging the polluted air of our ambitious illusions
Crying the dry tears of Beethoven's deafest masterpiece
We string together out of the tension
A landscape void of colour and text
Assembled by trembling hands as they withdraw

From the bottle in the left and the lover in the right
Where right is wrong and forgotten tears
Are smeared across kisses denied
Silent between heartbeats, where once
A piano kept the melody in playful time

Since elapsed like every great composer of eternal themes
Must perish beneath the conductor's wand
More violent and lyrical than our opening embrace
May have suggested
To our unsuspecting dreams.

Violent and Lyrical Embrace (continued)

Darkness on Mahler's Friday night dirge
Limping alone into the unfinished solo
Condemned to bleed its soul
Into a river unnamed, but for the suicides
Who have leapt into her toxic waves

A cry is chanted between violins
Who once held tune with compassion
For those who whispered dreams above their heads
Until hope, her strings snapped,
Broke the dual and only death

Unobserved,
Required a royal seal to proclaim
That we once lived.
And now we don't.
No one remains to gather the ashes and dust.

Autumn Grace

The Luxury of a garden lunch
Beneath a vast blue décor:

> The final ears of spinach, crisp to the cold;
> Hearty peppers suggest the need for a warmer coat
> Boiling potatoes and carrots
> Arouse the final embers
> That will embrace another night.

Creatures abound:

> Those in for the long haul
> Of cold and windy nights
> Fresh songs of hidden voices
> Among barely clad limbs

The quickly dissipating sun:

> Not exhausted, exactly,
> But lacking the fiery truth
> That once burned in summer veins.

Autumn Grace (continued)

The global touch of Autumn Grace:

> Just arriving at the chapel on the mountain
> Well rehearsed, spectacular in its subtlety.

None of us may merely witness:

> All of us
> Sing too our songs
> Brew too our soups
> Change too our colours
> Fall to our knees
> In humble awe of Autumn
> Being, within.

Healing Solitude

A hundred years on the cold face of this mountain
Since any man has tramped his urban feet along this wild path
Ashes and bones lay eroding, undisturbed
Gathering the magnificent solitude
Where I unveil the shroud of my soul before
The ancient glaciers at the distant reach of the valley
And sit in peace among the merciless thistles
That perforate my silent nest

A deferential village stretches into the valley
Horses, gardens and adobe homes
While to the *Mountain of the Cross*
I trust along the path where only goats have braved
In their tracks I seek the hidden rectitude of eternal peace
That cities cannot afford

Only in seclusion
Measured by forgetful space and deep trenches of time
May I truly nourish my heart
For in the comfort of society or my lover's arms
I am warmed and nurtured but never truly healed

Only in the cradle of the mountain,
Its rocky, impermeable trails,
Can I transcend this human vessel and encounter
The expansive world of the universe that I am
And here I laugh, for after all these incarnations
I still do not know my essential name

This existential void through which I wander
Seeking the tonic of infinite solitude
Where the heart of the mountain releases its anguish
And water falls under a different guise
Shadows cast their own peculiar beliefs
While thunder rolls a private drum
Goats straddle vertical cliffs, serpentine through the hills
I perch the shadow of my anonymous soul
Writhing with human convention and noise
Ever a stranger, homeless
But for this frail body that everyone believes to be me

Runaway Train

Thoughts stampede along abandoned rails
Penetrating
Nowhere
Forever
Into the everlasting abyss of the present
Rhythmically flowing
Without motion
Ever deeper into the here
The empty everywhere
The mind a runaway train
Connecting towns of ghosts and fields of grass
One blade resting on the other
A smile and a wink
A whiskeyed frown
The trains that depart from history
Are invisible in the now
And the here is ever still

History's less than Elegant Grace
(Huchuy Cusco, Perú)

Poetry has been tossed into crumbles
Like the collapsed walls of a long forgotten empire
Its stoic boulders lay strewn across hills in dark disarray

Salvation arrives with archaeological teams
Intoxicated with dreams of unearthing truth
Reconstructing words and walls from an ancient well

Poetry is resuscitated from shattered barbs
Excavated from dusty Incan ruins
Shredded by history's less than elegant Grace

The Andes wither so gradually as to never grey
Whereas old poets wrinkle and fade beneath the sun

In Defiance of Definition

What we think we know from our experience of time
Perpetuates that paradigm of the world
As we conceive, and thus, perceive it to be

All knowledge ages like deforested skulls
Concepts and facts go stale, not from lack of use,
But from perpetual familiarity

The drifter departs from the known
And seeks the outer reaches of the planet
Warm or cold, rags or gold

Searching beyond the stretch of all the words
In a language that promises to betray fulfilment
Of its own prophecies

The rambler sifts through idioms and vistas,
Tragedies and unstrung guitars
To welcome an eccentric being into existence

When the strings of a new day can be tightened and tuned
To articulate unwritten tongues
And tickle the distance of history

In Defiance of Definition (continued)

To reveal the boldest designs in meadows of thought
That we once claimed to know.
Now we ask afresh:

> *What is love without Grace?*
> *Electronic Friendship?*
> *War on War?*

Attend to this calling
For timeless awareness of Luxuries of Grace
To explore a world

Stampeding in defiance from all definitions
That humans have ever staked
Into the soil.

> *Poetry appears to be language*
> *While in truth,*
> *It is courage*

Signatures of Grace

Every creature leaves its distinct signature on the universe
Be it the jaguar's muddy footprint in the jungle
Or the monarch's golden brushstroke across the sky
We each, one by one, endorse our existence
On the dotted line assigned to us at birth

As signatures gather and regal petition becomes law
Our world is inspired to evolve from boiling lava
Into trembling mountains
        And finally
                Into scattered stones

By the time history arrives at the present moment
We must page through legions of names and places
Colours and dreams
Before we tentatively sign away our lives
To state in no uncertain terms
We have lived; we have existed.

In between, we make certain claims to truth
And a variety of half-truths that will largely be left unresolved
By the time our signatures fade from memory, into dust.

Signatures of Grace are organized by principles
Beyond the earthly grasp
But in one of our futures
The dots will connect and the stars
Will reveal our sacred destinies

We retain the hope that others will glean
A little insight from the reflections we have striven so hard
To embellish on the fossilized remains of the earth

Index of Poems

Alien Rhythms, 9
Apple of the Story, The, 15
Armless Weaver's Transcendent Loom, 1
Autumn Grace, 90
Barren Soil, 83
Being the Poem, 87
Bicycle Tour, 22
Confidence of Summer, The, 53
Current of Knowing, The, 12
Death Wish of a Stillborn Soul, 70
Defiance of Definition, In, 96
Divine Song of Morning Birds, 68
Dust of Violins, The, 10
Faithful Silence, 41
Fire Burns, not Knowing, 60
Fire on the Edge of the World, 36
First Quote of the Future, 82
Flowers and Stones Weave Colours for All, 59
Fresh, Bloody Shave, A, 75
Genetic Piñata, The, 56
Geology's Infamous Gaze, 80
Grizzly in the Closet, 71
Hardest Stone, The, 34
Harp of Autumn, 58
Healers and Madmen, 13
Healing of Poetry, The, 62
Healing Solitude, 92
Heart of Silence, In the, 50
History's less than Elegant Grace, 95
Ineffable Grace, 86
Inverse-Square Law of Gravity, The, 11
Lexicon of Innovation, The, 69
Listening to the River, 20
Little Death for Everyone, A, 49

Index of Poems (continued)

Loneliness of Truth, The, 4
Luxuries of Grace, 2
Memories of the Sun, 73
Memory Wavers high in the Andean Breeze, 21
Moments of Balance, 54
Morning's Cup of Tea, This, 16
Murder Variations, 46
Music by which to Destroy the World, 38
Music for Flamingos, 28
Nudge, The, 55
Nurture the Children of the Sun, To, 47
Om-niscience of Green, 37
Painter on the Esplanade, 18
Patching the Roof, 67
Peacocks within Stone, 72
Poetry Market, The, 43
Poetry Season, The 40
Quantum Search, 17
Raise the Ancient Rainbows, 30
Return of the Unshaven Poet, 48
Runaway Train, 94
Secrets of the Acorn, 64
Signature of my Soul is a Poem, The, 25
Signatures of Grace, 98
Silence between the Leaves, 79
Silence is Wiser than Thought, 61
Song of the Andes, 42
Soul of Music, The, 3
Sovereign Word, 5
Streetscape, La Paz, 6
Sustainable Breath, 35
Tears of the Sun, 66
Thorns of Scrubby Existence, 74
To Shine, to Be, 52

Index of Poems (continued)

Uncanny Mutations of Comprehension, 78
Violent and Lyrical Embrace, 88
Vision is Poetry, 14
Waves of Silence on the Island of the Sun, 76
Weathering, 81
What is the Essence of the Universe? 51
When Flight Chose Birds to Grace the Skies, 26
When to the River, 84
Where Born the Wind Was, 32
Whispers from the Inkwell, 31
White Rose of Friendship, 24
Wildflower, 27
Within the Empanadas, 44

About the Author

Tom Radzienda is a *Reiki* master and teacher in Thailand where he hosts an international healing centre. Previously, he was Assistant Professor at Srinakharinwirot University in Bangkok where he taught Western culture and literature from 1994 to 2006. During that time, he published three collections of poetry: *No More Pretty Pictures*, *A Promise for Siam* and *Fire Dreams*.

In 1999, he exhibited his photography and poetry to fund the *African Rhythms Friendship Project* to provide books for Iluya Primary School in Kenya. He has also combined poetry, photography and volunteer projects to support *Bahn Khru Noi* children's home in Bangkok.

Tom served as columnist for the *Bangkok Post* from 2000 to 2005. His column *Poet's Post* featured poetry and photography while *Poet Tree* instructed students and teachers in the arts of reading, writing and living a life of poetry.

In 2006, he served as a volunteer healer at *Mosoq Runa* children's home in Urubamba, Perú. In 2007 and 2008, he was a volunteer *Reiki* teacher and healer at *Moo Bahn Dek* Children's Village in Kanjanaburi, Thailand. Since 2008 he has been teaching *Reiki*, providing healing and counselling at his school/clinic in Bangkok.

Tom is the founder of the *Organic Reiki Ashram* in Chiang Mai in northern Thailand and is the author of *Personal Transformation through Reiki*. He has practised *Vipassana* meditation, Yoga, Vegetarianism and Naturopathy for many years. He combines these techniques with *Reiki* to the optimum benefit of each student.

He can be reached by email at tomradzienda@gmail.com